CHOOSE YOUR TOP 3

*500 Dynamic Discussion Starters to Get
Your Teenagers Talking*

Brian Schulenburg

Quick Questions

3,000?

CHOOSE
YOUR TOP

3

500 Dynamic Discussion Starters to Get Your Teenagers Talking

Brian Schulenburg

ZONDERVAN®

GRAND RAPIDS, MICHIGAN 49530

ZONDERVAN.COM/
AUTHOR**TRACKER**

Youth Specialties

www.youthspecialties.com

Youth Specialties

Choose Your Top 3...
500 Dynamic Discussion Starters to Get Your Teenagers Talking
Copyright © 2006 by Brian Schulenburg

Youth Specialties products, 300 South Pierce Street, El Cajon, CA 92020 are published by Zondervan, 5300 Patterson Avenue Southeast, Grand Rapids, MI 49530.

Library of Congress Cataloging-in-Publication Data

Schulenburg, Brian.
  Choose your top 3-- : 500 dynamic discussion starters to get your teenagers talking / Brian Schulenburg.
    p. cm.
  ISBN-10: 0-310-26746-3 (pbk.)
  ISBN-13: 978-0-310-26746-1 (pbk.)
  1. Church work with teenagers. I. Title: Choose your top three--. II. Title.
  BV4447.S295 2006
  268'.433--dc22

                                                                    2006003987

Creative team: Dave Urbanski and Vicki Newby
Cover design: Holly Sharp

Printed in the United States

---

06 07 08 09 10 • 10 9 8 7 6 5 4 3 2 1

DEDICATION

This book is dedicated to the love of my life. Cyndi, I love you. Thank you for the 17 years that you've spent with me. Thank you for believing in me. You are grace and peace. You are my joy and delight. You are wise, and you are beautiful. I am blessed.

TABLE OF CONTENTS

Acknowledgments   9

Introduction   11

How to Use *Choose Your Top 3...*   13

All 500 *Choose Your Top 3...* Items   17

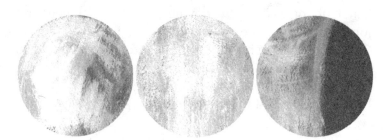

ACKNOWLEDGMENTS

No book can ever be written without the input and advice of numerous people. Thanks to Jay Howver, Dave Urbanski, and Roni Meek of Youth Specialties for the faith that they had in this project and for their editorial prowess. Thank you to Vicki Newby for the great job she did editing my manuscript and to Heather Haggerty for proofreading it. Thanks to Holly Sharp for designing an incredible cover.

Thanks to Tom Thoresen, a friend who helped my editorial time go by so much faster after a name change on this project.

Thank you to Faith Evangelical Presbyterian Church in Alexandria, Virginia, First Evangelical Free Church in Moline, Illinois, and Wooddale Church in Eden Prairie, Minnesota; all have allowed me to serve on their church staffs as a pastor to students.

Finally, thank you to the following people who contributed questions to this book: Cyndi Schulenburg, Breanna Schulenburg, Christopher Schulenburg, Jeremy

Schulenburg, Zachary Schulenburg, Gordon Schulenburg, Jon Agrimson, Susie Anderson, Sarah Bancroft, Rachel Cramer, Diane Dahl, Kara Doten, Amy Emerson, Kaila Fagerstrom, Sara Geis, Ryan Greene, Peter Gosen, Danielle Iskierka, Tim Langefels, Sarah Oehrig, Justin Satterberg, Pete Swanson, and Carrie Youngblood.

INTRODUCTION

An old Chinese proverb says, "One who asks a question is a fool for five minutes; one who does not ask a question remains a fool forever."

For years the Quick Questions Library from Youth Specialties has been equipping youth workers with questions to give insight into the students we work with. Questions are one of the greatest tools we have for bridging the relational gap between individuals. My prayer is that *Choose Your Top 3...* will help you understand your students as never before.

The questions in this book will bring out a wide range of emotions in them. Some questions are tough; your students will have to think quite a while before coming up with three answers. Some questions will make students laugh as they remember humorous times from years ago or listen to their peers' answers. Some questions will make students think deeply regarding their beliefs about God.

My prayer is that these questions will help you discover previously hidden areas in your students' lives—they very well could delight you, shock you, teach you, and drive you to your knees. Hopefully they'll propel you with even greater resolve to be part of this thing we call student ministry.

May God bless you, fellow youth worker, on your journey through the world of students.

In Him,

Brian Schulenburg
Eden Prairie, Minnesota

E-mail your *Choose Your Top 3* ideas to: brian_schulenburg@yahoo.com

The best ideas will be periodically posted on
Brian's blog: *http://bschulenburg.blogspot.com*.

HOW TO USE *CHOOSE YOUR TOP 3 . . .*

Choose Your Top 3... is a discussion starter, a tool for you to get your kids talking. Here are a few suggestions for how and when to use it:

Random Questions

Some youth workers like to get students to pick a number between one and 500 when using the Youth Specialties Quick Questions books. Students love being asked random questions.

Specific Questions Selected in Advance

You may have a particular theme you're teaching. Skim through the questions and find some that fit the topic. Or you may have a specific student who comes to mind as you read a certain question. Write the student's initials in pencil next to the question, and ask her the question the next time you have an event.

Road Trips

Let your radio station arguments end on your next road trip. Bring this book along and let the conversation roll. You'll be amazed at how much faster the road trip goes when you get students talking. Bring along other Youth Specialties Quick Questions books. Mix it up and ask the questions from several books.

Campfires

No retreat is complete without a campfire. While time around the campfire at the end of the retreat is usually spent talking about ways God worked during the previous few days, an earlier campfire is a prime opportunity for using *Choose Your Top 3...* You'll gain insights into your students and have information for starting conversations that you can use during the rest of your time with them.

Classrooms

This book can be used in church and school classrooms. Use the book as part of your opening time. Students will look forward to coming into the room and finding out more about each other.

Small Groups

Throw a few of these questions into the mix before you begin your small group discussion in earnest. The questions can prime your group to get the conversation rolling.

And remember, if you have small group leaders working alongside you, some might want help leading conversations and getting kids talking. This book is a great tool to share with your small group leaders.

Important caveat: Make sure you read the questions before using them with your students.

Some questions may be inappropriate for particular students. It would be entirely out of line to ask a student who has never met his or her father to "Choose your top three qualities that you admire most about your dad." You could revise the question so it's about another male influence in the student's life, such as a volunteer in your youth ministry.

Some questions may be inappropriate for the sensitivities of your church or community. If asking about

Halloween or tattoos could cost you your position, make sure you skip or revise those.

I'd love to hear how you are using *Choose Your Top 3...* in your ministry setting. Send me an e-mail at brian_schulenburg@yahoo.com. God bless you, and happy questioning!

1 . . . vacation destinations.

2 . . . TV comedies.

3 . . . pizza toppings.

4 . . . most influential people in your life.

5 . . . cars.

6 . . . books of the Bible.

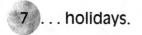 . . . holidays.

8 . . . summer Olympic events.

9 . . . super powers (X-ray vision, ability to fly, etc.).

10 . . . most beautiful people you've ever met.

11 . . . animated cartoon characters.

12 . . . clothing brands.

13 . . . things you'd miss if you lost your
eyesight for the rest of your life.

14 . . . qualities you respect about your parents.

15 . . . U.S. presidents.

16 . . . cola flavors (e.g., cherry, vanilla, lemon,
lime, diet, etc.).

 . . . stores in the mall closest to your home.

. . . movies of all time.

 . . . questions about God.

20 . . . teachers you've ever had.

21 . . . most-listened-to songs on your MP3 player.

22 . . . childhood toys.

 . . . places you'd like to go on a mission trip.

24 . . . meals your family eats at home.

25 . . . sports to watch.

26 . . . decades you'd want to live in.

27 . . . types of fruit.

28 . . . insects.

29 . . . reasons to go out on a date.

 **30** . . . problems the world's youth face today.

 31 . . . comedians.

32 . . . excuses for not turning in homework.

33 . . . books of all time.

 34 . . . sit-down restaurants.

 35 . . . amusement park rides.

36 . . . qualities you look for in a presidential candidate.

37 . . . crayon colors.

38 . . . male actors.

39 . . . musical instruments.

40 . . . activities you've done with your youth group.

41 . . . pro baseball teams.

42 . . . Bible verses.

43 . . . smart people.

44 . . . hip-hop songs.

45 . . . salad dressings.

46 ... traits you admire in the youth group leaders at your church.

47 ... farm animals.

48 ... sandwiches.

49 ... things you'd change about your church.

50 ... authors.

51 . . . reality-TV shows.

52 . . . ways you've served your community.

53 . . . high school subcultures (jocks, Goths, preps, etc.).

54 . . . things you like about summer.

55 . . . states in the U.S.

56 . . . famous quotations.

57 . . . Star Wars movies.

 58 . . . Internet sites.

59 . . . people in your youth group most likely to become president of the United States.

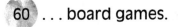 **60** . . . board games.

. . . things that scare you about sharing your faith.

 . . . qualities you like about your family.

63 . . . items in your closet.

 . . . ice cream flavors.

65 . . . problems or injustices that make you angry.

66 . . . spiritual gifts.

67 . . . traits you want in a future spouse.

68 . . . memories from kindergarten.

69 . . . inventions that changed the world.

70 . . . winter Olympic events.

71 . . . kinds of chocolate.

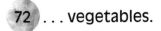

 72 . . . vegetables.

73 . . . reasons for not inviting a friend to church.

74 . . . countries in the world.

75 . . . spring break destinations.

 76 . . . school cafeteria meals.

77 . . . school subjects.

78 . . . places you would most hate to live.

79 . . . TV moms.

80 . . . female singers.

81 . . . ways you like to spend time with God.

82 . . . gifts you've received.

83 . . . Internet search engines.

84 . . . cities in the world.

85 . . . fast-food restaurants.

86 . . . qualities or activities you like about your church.

87 . . . things you like about prayer.

88 . . . ways teachers have influenced you.

89 . . . careers you'd like to pursue.

90 . . . colleges.

91 . . . branches of the military.

92 . . . attributes of God.

93 . . . uniforms of pro sports teams.

94 . . . dog names.

95 . . . male singers.

96 . . . donuts.

97 . . . beaches.

98 . . . colors in the rainbow.

99 . . . qualities you look for in a friend.

100 . . . most terrifying experiences in your life.

101 . . . school field trip locations.

102 . . . soups.

103 . . . Halloween costumes.

104 . . . most painful places to have a bruise.

105 . . . pet peeves.

106 . . . radio stations.

 107 . . . countries you'd most like to visit.

 108 . . . worst-tasting medicines.

 109 . . . places to order French fries.

 110 . . . things you'd miss if you lost the ability
to hear for the rest of your life.

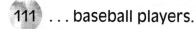

111 ... baseball players.

112 ... benefits of the Internet.

113 ... potato chip flavors.

114 ... ways to celebrate New Year's Eve.

115 ... people you want to emulate.

 116 ... TV commercials.

117 . . . ways to prepare an egg.

118 . . . outdoor activities.

119 . . . sports teams.

120 . . . country songs.

 121 . . . condiments.

 122 . . . video games.

123　. . . charities.

124　. . . DVD extras.

125　. . . things that scare you about being a
　　　pastor or missionary.

126　. . . birds.

127　. . . people who have had worldwide
　　　influence.

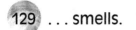 **128** . . . concerts you've attended.

 129 . . . smells.

 130 . . . people in your youth group most likely to become college professors.

131 . . . pizza joints.

 132 . . . cookie flavors.

133 . . . Bible characters.

134 . . . nail polish colors.

135 . . . famous people you'd like to meet.

136 . . . sayings of Jesus.

137 . . . types of weather.

138 . . . TV dads.

. . . musical groups from the 1980s.

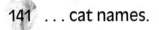 . . . Disney princesses.

141 . . . cat names.

 . . . Batman villains.

 . . . questions you want to ask God when you get to heaven.

. . . politicians.

 . . . female actors.

 . . . video game systems.

144 . . . memories with your mom.

 . . . professional wrestlers.

149 . . . nicknames for your friends.

. . . fairy tales.

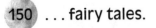 . . . people in your youth group most likely
         to become professional athletes.

 . . . fears.

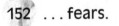 . . . personal injury stories (broken bones,
         stitches, etc.).

 . . . qualities you like about yourself.

155 . . . causes you are passionate about.

156 . . . days of the week.

 157 . . . qualities you like about babies.

158 . . . sporting events.

159 . . . places to shop for a prom dress.

160 . . . types of shoes.

161 . . . Christian music groups.

 162 . . . baby food flavors.

 163 . . . Disney movies.

 164 . . . things your parents do that bug you.

165 . . . qualities you admire most about your dad.

166   . . . places to go for fun.

167   . . . memories with your grandparents.

168   . . . candy bars.

169   . . . gum flavors.

170   . . . pro basketball players.

171   . . . lake trip activities.

. . . fruit juices.

 . . . qualities you admire about your pastor.

174 . . . toughest subjects in school.

175 . . . television networks.

 . . . presents you've given to other people.

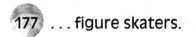 . . . figure skaters.

178 . . . embarrassing moments.

179 . . . Julia Roberts movies.

180 . . . stage plays you've seen.

181 . . . musicals.

182 . . . wonders of the world.

183 . . . questions about outer space.

. . . TV talk shows.

 . . . card games.

 . . . events you'd like to experience in your lifetime (walk on the moon, attend a royal wedding, etc.).

 . . . places to go on a church retreat.

188 . . . superheroes.

189 . . . people in your youth group most likely
          to become pastors.

190 . . . questions you have about Islam.

191 . . . exotic locations.

192 . . . ocean creatures.

193 . . . football players.

194 . . . places to go for an inexpensive date.

 195 . . . qualities you admire most about your mom.

 196 . . . hobbies.

 197 . . . movies about high school.

198 . . . possessions that have sentimental value to you.

199 . . . news stories of all time.

200 . . . Bible stories.

201 . . . moments in history.

202 . . . things you'd be willing to stand in line for two hours to buy.

203 . . . TV shows of all time.

204 . . . cake flavors.

 205 . . . sacrifices that your parents have made for you.

 206 . . . difficult homework assignments.

 207 . . . family traditions.

 208 . . . household chores.

209 . . . words in the English language.

210 . . . ways to exercise.

211 . . . Christmas movies.

212 . . . social issues you'd like solved in your lifetime.

213 . . . ways to travel.

. . . reasons to like Thanksgiving.

 . . . pro hockey teams.

216 . . . movies that you would like to have starred in.

 . . . jellybean flavors.

 . . . positions on a football team.

219 . . . types of jewelry.

220 . . . books from your childhood.

221 . . . months of the year.

222 . . . ideas your pastor has told you.

223 . . . pranks others have played on you.

224 . . . pranks you've played on others.

225 . . . craziest things you've done in your life.

 226 . . . joyful people.

 227 . . . types of bread.

 228 . . . possessions you wish you had never thrown away.

 229 . . . causes of stress.

230 . . . reasons to look forward to tomorrow.

231 . . . promises from the Bible.

232 . . . qualities you like about your bedroom.

233 . . . circus acts.

234 . . . world leaders.

235 . . . zoo animals.

. . . oldest possessions.

 . . . movie villains.

 . . . coaches.

 . . . traits you admire about police officers and fire fighters.

 . . . people in your youth group most likely to become CEOs of major computer companies.

241 . . . places to get photos developed.

242 . . . pictures you've taken.

243 . . . skills you possess.

244 . . . monuments to see in Washington, D.C.

245 . . . team mascots.

246 . . . types of cheese.

247 . . . romantic comedy movies.

 248 . . . people in your youth group most likely to make world-changing discoveries.

 249 . . . places you'd like to go on a shopping spree.

 250 . . . grossest things you've ever done.

 251 . . . numbers.

252 . . . TV police shows.

253 . . . activities that take place on ice.

254 . . . college football teams.

255 . . . fast-food dollar-menu items.

256 . . . pieces of advice people have given to
       you about relationships.

. . . types of pets.

 . . . books you'd like turned into movies.

 . . . items you'd purchase if given $10,000 to spend however you want.

 . . . Charlie Brown cartoons.

 . . . names of God.

262 . . . Christian colleges or universities.

263 . . . praise and worship or gospel songs.

264 . . . reasons for not becoming a missionary
        to Africa.

265 . . . traits you like about senior citizens.

266 . . . C. S. Lewis books.

267 . . . experiences you want to try within the next 10 years.

 268 . . . reasons for not spending time in retirement homes.

 269 . . . pieces of advice people have given you about money.

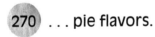 270 . . . pie flavors.

 271 . . . questions about hell.

272 . . . service projects you've participated in.

273 . . . boy bands.

274 . . . foods to grill.

275 . . . qualities about the Fourth of July.

276 . . . most embarrassing reasons to see a doctor.

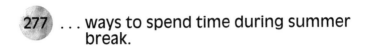 **277** . . . ways to spend time during summer break.

 **278** . . . people in your youth group most likely to become professional wrestlers.

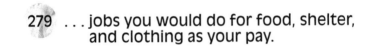 **279** . . . jobs you would do for food, shelter, and clothing as your pay.

 280 . . . ways to spend a Friday night.

 281 . . . school rivals.

282 . . . things that scare you about being in the Armed Forces.

283 . . . musical groups.

 284 . . . wishes if a genie could make them come true.

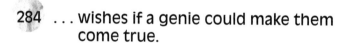 285 . . . ice cream toppings.

 286 . . . places you'd like to raise a family.

287   ... things you don't want to live without.

288   ... things you pray for.

289   ... sports movies.

290   ... unusual names.

291   ... pieces of furniture in your home.

292   ... water sports.

293 . . . sermons you've heard.

294 . . . stuffed animals from your childhood.

295 . . . ministries you wish your church would start.

296 . . . meals you've eaten.

297 . . . people in your youth group most likely to sing the national anthem at the Super Bowl.

298 . . . perfumes.

299 . . . fears about the future.

300 . . . comic books.

301 . . . U.S. coins.

302 . . . ways to send a package.

303 . . . items in your locker.

304 . . . milkshake flavors.

305 . . . blue jean brands.

306 . . . reasons for not doing your homework.

307 . . . people in your youth group most likely
to become Broadway stars.

308 . . . reasons for having devotions.

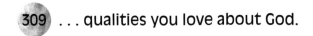

 309 . . . qualities you love about God.

 310 . . . breath mint brands.

311 . . . reasons for not using instant messaging.

312 . . . worst fads.

 313 . . . musical groups from the 1990s.

 . . . college majors.

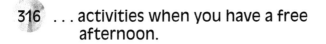 . . . reasons to not pursue a career in farming.

 . . . activities when you have a free afternoon.

317 . . . items you look for at garage sales.

 . . . scariest bugs.

319 . . . TV families.

320 . . . music videos.

321 . . . memories from your last vacation.

322 . . . appetizers at your favorite restaurant.

323 . . . games to play during PE.

324 . . . movie quotations.

325 . . . animals that fly.

326 . . . reasons to enjoy a thunderstorm.

327 . . . people in your youth group most likely to appear on TV dating shows.

328 . . . friends' homes you'd want to live in.

329 . . . longest road trips.

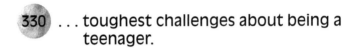

 ... toughest challenges about being a teenager.

 ... Mexican foods.

 ... things you dislike about the last presidential election.

333 ... Christmas carols.

 ... places to buy a hamburger.

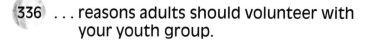

335 . . . diseases you hope will be cured in your lifetime.

336 . . . reasons adults should volunteer with your youth group.

337 . . . CDs you want to purchase.

338 . . . movie sequels.

339 . . . people who've shown you love.

340 . . . national monuments.

341 . . . games to play in a car.

342 . . . types of trees.

343 . . . questions about the Book of Revelation.

344 . . . guitarists.

345 ... ways that your church is making an impact on its community.

346 ... war movies.

347 ... reasons to defend your view of the Earth's age.

348 ... taco toppings.

349 ... European cities.

350 ... types of fish to catch.

351 ... heavy metal songs.

352 ... facial features.

353 ... reasons to like or hate NASCAR.

354 ... mysteries about the Holy Spirit.

355 ... popcorn flavors.

356 . . . next movies that should be nominated for Best Picture Academy Awards.

357 . . . people you'd like to kiss.

358 . . . worst pizza toppings.

359 . . . lollipop flavors.

360 . . . coffee shop drinks.

361 . . . cereals.

 362 . . . things you'd miss if you lost the ability to speak for the rest of your life.

 363 . . . car colors.

 364 . . . state license plates.

365 . . . comfort foods.

366 . . . violations committed at your school.

367 . . . worst punishments you have received.

368 . . . character flaws.

369 . . . blunders you won't make when you're raising your own kids.

370 . . . events you wish you could do over.

371 . . . U.S. cities.

372 . . . qualities you'd never change about yourself.

373 . . . Arnold Schwarzenegger movies.

374 . . . qualities about Easter.

375 . . . milk flavors.

376 ... things you would never be caught doing.

377 ... places you would hate to work as an intern.

378 ... reasons to break up.

379 ... magazines.

380 ... funny names in the Bible.

 . . . worst inventions.

382 . . . rules you'd like your school to abolish.

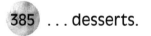 . . . things that bug you about the Bible.

384 . . . sandwich meats.

385 . . . desserts.

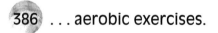 . . . aerobic exercises.

387 . . . pro basketball teams.

388 . . . parables.

389 . . . qualities you like about your principal.

390 . . . water park rides.

391 . . . qualities you like about the job your
mom or dad has.

392 ... movie theaters.

393 ... movie-rental stores.

394 ... types of fireworks.

395 ... schools you've attended.

396 ... types of flowers.

397 ... pasta dishes.

398 . . . memories with your dad.

399 . . . historical eras.

400 . . . photos in your photo albums.

401 . . . worst movie sequels.

402 . . . awards you've received.

403 . . . senses.

404 . . . items to look for in an antique store.

405 . . . possessions you'd like to sell on eBay.

406 . . . characters from the Star Wars movies.

407 . . . things you'd do if you suddenly inherited $1 million.

408 . . . ways you could help a homeless person.

409 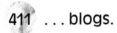 . . . traditions of your church.

410 . . . qualities about Mother Teresa.

411 . . . blogs.

412 . . . pro football quarterbacks.

413 . . . reasons for not supporting a child from an underdeveloped nation.

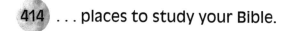

414 ... places to study your Bible.

415 ... worst colors to wear to a funeral.

416 ... adventure trips you'd like to take.

417 ... issues in the Middle East to pray for.

418 ... embarrassing things other Christians do or say.

419 . . . comments you would like to tell your
     pastor.

420 . . . discoveries you would like to make.

421 . . . things that scared you when you were
     alone in the dark as a little child.

422 . . . worst household chores.

423 . . . things you'd miss if you spent the rest
     of your life in a wheelchair.

424 . . . places you'd like to spend your honeymoon.

425 . . . sports skills you want to improve.

426 . . . characters from Snow White and the Seven Dwarfs.

427 . . . drinks to quench your thirst.

428 . . . people you wouldn't want seeing you kissing your boyfriend/girlfriend.

429 . . . Popsicle flavors.

430 . . . Christmas ornaments.

431 . . . pro hockey players.

432 . . . cell phone features.

433 . . . chick flicks.

434 . . . electronics you'd like to own.

435 . . . hair colors.

436 . . . dog breeds.

437 . . . qualities in a boss.

438 . . . breakfast foods.

439 . . . paintings.

440 . . . personality traits.

441 . . . excuses for skipping school.

 442 . . . pieces of playground equipment.

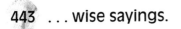 443 . . . wise sayings.

444 . . . speakers to invite to your next youth group retreat.

445 . . . letters of the alphabet.

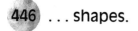 446 . . . shapes.

447 . . . ways you've been surprised.

448 . . . birthday memories.

449 . . . Christmas gifts.

450 . . . items to collect (baseball cards, coins, etc.).

451 . . . personal achievements.

452 . . . snack foods.

453 . . . miracles in the Bible.

454 . . . pro football teams.

455 . . . locations where you've attended a
wedding reception.

456 . . . colors you'd like the walls in your room to be.

 **457** . . . angel stories from the Bible.

 458 . . . rap songs.

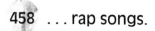 **459** . . . ways someone has shown you love.

 460 . . . sections of the newspaper.

461 . . . power tools.

462 . . . celebrity marriages.

463 . . . movies you'd like to see at a drive-in theater.

464 . . . people in your youth group most likely to have art on display in the Louvre.

465 . . . classical music composers.

466 . . . TV Christmas specials.

467 . . . places to go camping.

468 . . . makeup brands.

469 . . . Lord of the Rings characters.

470 . . . salty-sweet food combinations.

471 . . . autumn activities.

472 . . . fashion designers.

473 . . . restaurants to eat ribs.

474 . . . people you like to hug.

475 . . . muscles.

476 . . . moments you want to relive.

477 . . . people who make you laugh.

478 . . . effective cold remedies.

479 . . . planets you'd like to visit.

480 . . . puking memories.

481 . . . spots on your body for a tattoo.

482 . . . positions to sleep in.

483 . . . laughs of people you know.

484 . . . activities you wish your church would offer.

485 . . . drama or action movies.

486 . . . artistic skills you want to improve (singing, playing an instrument, etc.).

487 . . . animals that live in the ocean.

488 . . . ways to get around without a motor.

489 . . . school supplies you couldn't live without (stapler, three-hole punch, etc.).

 490 . . . cable TV stations.

 491 . . . comic strip characters.

 492 . . . disciples of Jesus.

493 . . . people who offer advice.

494 . . . ways you'd like to change.

495 . . . responsibilities you're glad your parents have instead of you.

496 . . . languages you wish you could speak fluently.

497 . . . clothing accessories.

498 . . . women in the Bible.

499 . . . writing utensils.

 500 . . . ideas for the next *Choose Your Top 3 . . .* book.